Escape From The Bad Life

# ESCAPE FROM THE BAD LIFE

*One Gangster's Path of Discovery to Freedom*

by Santo Grasso

SET
FREE
SOLDIERS.
ORG
PUBLISHER

*For information, contact:*
SetFreeSoldiers.org
3001 Spring Valley Road
Charlotte, NC 28210

*Printed In the United States of America*
First edition

Cover and book layout by gary hixson

ISBN 978-0-578-19011-2

This book is dedicated to
Chaplin Bevans, Santo, Sr., and
Annie and Harold Wheeler,
*with thanks to*
*gary hixson and my wife Nicole*

# TABLE OF CONTENTS

Escape From The Bad Life

Escape From The Bad Life

# INTRODUCING ME

### Who am I and why read this book?

Born and raised in Baltimore by my Father and Grandmother, I was well cared for and given many opportunities. Basically, I was your average "good kid" who never really got into trouble.

However, I wasn't average in everything, however. I was a standout basketball player, and was eventually selected as an All-American, which led to my playing in the McDonald's Classic basketball game, and meeting President Reagan (along with all of my teammates).

After high school, I was offered several basketball scholarships for College. I chose Notre Dame University, and then Mount St. Mary's University in Maryland.

After attending for several months, I started feeling restless and unfulfilled, so I dropped out. Higher education just wasn't for me.

It wasn't long before I started getting into trouble. Before long, I became attached to the motorcycle gang lifestyle and moved to California.

Eventually, I was accepted as a member in one of the world's deadliest motorcycle gangs, and quickly rose through the ranks. I served as a Gang Enforcer, and later became their East Coast Boss, returning to Baltimore. By the age of 25 I had become a millionaire, and one of the most wanted criminals in the country.

I was featured on "America's Most Wanted," "Gangland" and "The History Channel." Eventually, the ATF, FBI, IRS charged me with tax evasion and fraud, and I was convicted and went to a maximum security Federal prison for 3(?) years, where I spent 23 hours of every day locked up alone.

Another inmate started asking questions I couldn't answer and then gave me a Bible, which I had no interest in. But since I had nothing else to do, I read it, and eventually, to my surprise (and the profound disbelief of others who knew me), I actually became a devoted believer in Jesus. I was a spiritual infant, for sure.

Upon my release, I returned briefly to Baltimore, where I attended a church and was baptized into Christ.

While I had been in prison, my Mother had relocated to North Carolina, so to avoid the negative influences of previous associates, that's where I went.

It was a good place for me to be, but I had lost all of the things I had long known, including the respect of others and my own self-respect. Understandably, I quickly became very depressed and isolated.

Not aware of it at the time, I was mourning the void that all my possessions, multiple homes and money had previously filled. So, to ease the pain of my emptiness, I turned to alcohol and drugs for the first time in my life, and was soon addicted.

Once I realized I couldn't escape my addiction on my own, I sought out help at an area addiction program, Rebound! for men at the Charlotte Rescue Mission, and later turned to the Promise Resource Network (PRN), also in Charlotte, both of which helped me understand myself and others in new and different ways.

Not long after, I was visiting a church in Texas, sitting on the front row, hungry to learn from the pastor.

After the worship, Pastor Duff approached me and said, "You have a halo over your head," and said that God had a calling for me, to help others out of bad spots into good spots – none of which I really understood as a baby Christian.

Then he surprised me further by saying, "You have five minutes to decide to be ordained as a minister." A deacon who was present briefly explained what a minister's role is, and I accepted the calling. That was in January of 2011. I left inspired to help others, but with little knowledge and a young faith, unsure how to proceed.

Today, I'm a card-carrying ordained Minister, have certifications in training of various kinds, and have started a non-profit ministry called "Set Free Soldiers." It serves people with dependencies and addictions, and who suffer with behavioral problems, and I currently serve as a "Be Set Free" Recovery Educator.

# PERSONAL ORIENTATION

If you're reading this book, you're undoubtedly searching for solutions. Your life, like every human life, is a collection of stories, some grand, some not-so-grand, some disappointing and some tragic.

During the good times, you will celebrate, but when tragedy comes, you will likely return to asking many of the same unanswered questions.

This book is intended to help you find answers.

Perhaps you have sought solutions on your own or from friends and family. Wherever you are, no matter how difficult your problem, I am convinced God has a plan for you, a plan that comforts, gives peace, joy and happiness. You can find it all in His Holy Word (the Bible) and, to a far lesser extent, this book, which is intended  to help you find your life's purpose and a rewarding (and sane) direction.

If/when you sincerely want to discover God's plan for your life, it will be up to you to learn your life's critical lessons. It will be up to you to make changes and choices that are pleasing to God (and that will ultimately bless your life).

One last thing before you go any farther – know that this is not a "how to" book.

I'm simply sharing highlights and insights I learned along the path of my own personal escape from a very bad life that was leading me nowhere.

I am genuinely hoping that these lessons are helpful as you consider making your escape.

# THE STRATEGY OF PATIENCE

In game play, it has always been my philosophy that patience will win out. By that I mean patience to follow your game plan. If you sincerely believe in your plan, you can wear the opponent down and get to them.

However, if you break away from your plan, and play their way or out of desperation to win, you will always be in trouble.

And if you let your emotions direct the way you play the game rather than your plan, then you will not function effectively.

If you play your game, you must stick to your style.

This does not mean that we will always win or outscore your opponent.

It does ensure that we will not beat ourselves.

Psalm 37 (*in the Old Testament part of the Bible*) says, in effect, "Do what is right and trust me."

Regardless of how badly you may seem to be losing, you will always be wise by just doing God's will and leaving the outcome to Him. He'll make sure that eventually you will be the winner. Such a strategy will not only keep us from beating ourselves, it will lead to glorious victory.

# LOOK WHO IS READING WHOM

It was a judge who used bumper stickers to encourage better driving. He gave two options to people who were guilty of driving while intoxicated.

The first option was to attach a message to their bumper that read, "This car owned by a convicted drunk driver." Almost all offenders preferred the second option – a bumper sticker that read "Enroll in AA."

The majority of people cared about what others thought of them and wanted to maintain a good image.

The fear of embarrassment applies to other kinds of negative and personally destructive behaviors, as well.

For example, not many of us would be willing to walk around with a sign on our back that reads something like this – "Danger: I'm a Christian who doesn't spend time in prayer or Bible study," "Warning: I am a child of God who gossips too much," or "Be careful, I am controlled by lust rather than love."

God requires us to display love, respect, strength, and the wisdom to know the Word of God. Our spiritual Father, God, is the only one who truly judges us. (1 Peter 1:17 *New Testament*). And He has paid an amazing price so that His ultimate judgment for our mistakes can be transferred onto His son, Jesus. Remember: Everyone else just has an opinion about us.

# SEEING OR REMEMBERING

There was a man who was slowly losing his memory. After an examination by his physician, the doctor said that an operation on his brain might reverse his condition and restore his memory. However, the surgery would be so delicate that a nerve might be severed causing total blindness.

The doctor asked, "Which would you rather have – no memory or total blindness?" The man pondered for a moment and then replied, "My sight, because I would rather see where I am going (than remember where I've been)."

In the third chapter of Philippians (*a letter to*

*believers found in the New Testament part of the Bible)* the apostle Paul made the same spiritual choice.

His past, with its success and shame is what he chose to lose. What mattered to him was keeping his eyes on the goal of gaining Christ's approval and the blessing living for him brings (Philippians 3:13-15).

# WE REAP WHAT WE SOW

Many of us are deeply troubled by the injustices we see in life, especially when the people who are most obviously ignoring God are often the ones who appear to be prospering the most.

But you can be sure of this – God is not mocked. For whatever a man sows he will also reap (Galatians 6:7 – *a New Testament letter*).

In Psalm 7 (*Old Testament*), a truth our short attention span can cause us to miss is revealed – sooner or later evildoers will reap what they sow. We have nothing to lose or fear if we sow what is good.

Centuries ago David, Kings of the Jews, wrote:

"Whoever is pregnant with evil conceives trouble and gives birth to disillusionment. Whoever digs a hole and scoops it out falls into the pit they have made. The trouble they cause recoils on them; their violence comes down on their own heads." (Psalm 7:14-16 *Old Testament*)

Still, there is hope for anyone who has been ignoring God up until now. In 2 Peter 3:8-9 (*New Testament*) it's written:

"But do not forget this one thing, dear friends: With the Lord a day is like a thousand years, and a thousand years are like a day. The Lord is not slow in keeping his promise, as some understand slowness. Instead he is patient with you, not wanting anyone to perish, but everyone to come to repentance."

# A ROLLER COASTER RIDE

If you love someone who struggles with substance abuse problems, then you already know that your and their lives and emotions can be like riding a roller coaster. Up and down. Jerked left and right. Loop after loop. Then repeat the ride.

Today he wants help, tomorrow he's drinking or high on drugs – again. Today she's being honest, and tomorrow she is running from the truth.

The Holy Spirit helps us learn how to love people like that, even in their sins and struggles.

Here are a few principles you can put practice:

• Treat the person with respect

• Be gentle when trying to restore them.

• Don't get in the way of the consequences that God can use to bring about change (Galatians 6:1 *New Testament*).

Remember that change can happen at any time. So, ask God to help you to reach out in love.

• Seek His wisdom in what to say during your interactions (James 1:5 *New Testament*).

• When appropriate, rebuke or be silent in love.

• Depend on God because you will make mistakes.

• Anchor yourself in God's Word and continually commit yourself and your love of the Lord in prayer (Philippians 4:6 *New Testament*).

Making these choices can help slow down life's roller coaster ride.

# A PLAN FOR US

I take walks on the city's railroad overpasses and in its parks. I am not looking for lost treasures. I am looking for homeless people.

That's how I met a guy named Frankie who was living in the park in the dead of winter, and he was mentally ill. I started talking with him and telling him about the gifts of God and God's love for each of us.

After meeting him, I would stop by occasionally to give him some food and clothes, and share the Word of God's treasure.

In Mark 10:21 (*New Testament*) Jesus teaches. "Sell whatever you have and give to the poor and you will have treasure in heaven. Come pick up the cross and follow me."

I soon realized that I had more in common with the Frankie than I'd first thought. The raw fact is that we are all spiritually bankrupt if we don't have Jesus in our heart.

One day, I asked Frankie if he'd like to go to church with me. That night, I got him a motel room so he could get a shower and a good night's rest. On Sunday I picked him up for church, and afterwards we got something to eat.

He started asking a lot of questions about God and how he can get "there." I took him step-by-step and showed him everything in the Bible that I could. I wanted to show him the way to spiritual blessing.

We talked for hours on end. He asked if I was going to church the next Sunday and I said, "Yes." I told him I would pick him up bright and early.

On that Sunday, the preacher talked about a lot of things that hit home for Frankie, because he started crying. He let his feelings come out, and I asked if he would like to give Jesus a try.

Frankie looked at me and said, "It can only get

better right, Santo?" And I said, "Yes."

So that day Frankie gave himself to Christ. After church we went out to eat and I took him back to his room at the motel. Frankie asked if he could join me for Bible Study that Wednesday and, of course, I said, "Yes, see you then."

That was the last time I would see or hear from Frankie. He died that Tuesday from a heart attack.

I believe God used me to get into Frankie's life, to help show him the way. One thing I know for sure – Frankie is with God in Heaven. He was saved on the last Sunday of his life.

Never give up on those you think are hopeless or homeless. They can still find hope and a safe place with God.

# HOW IS YOUR HEART?

"The eyes of the Lord are on the righteous,
and his ears are attentive to their cry."
Psalm 34:15 (*Old Testament*)

"Where can I go from your Spirit?
Where can I flee from your presence?
If I go up to the heavens, you are there;
if I make my bed in the depths, you are there.
If I rise on the wings of the dawn,
if I settle on the far side of the sea,
even there your hand will guide me,
your right hand will hold me fast.

If I say, 'Surely the darkness will hide me
and the light become night around me,'
even the darkness will not be dark to you;
the night will shine like the day,
for darkness is as light to you."
Psalm 139:7-12 (*Old Testament*)

I tend to focus on believing with my mind and working with my hands. In the activity of thinking and serving, my heart is pushed to the side. When Jesus told an illustration of how people received and responded to his teaching (Matthew 13:1-9 *New Testament*), his disciples asked why do you speak to them in parables.

In reply, Jesus quoted the prophet Isaiah – "For the hearts of his people have grown dull. Their ears are hard of hearing and their eyes are closed."

The more they heard and had not seen with their eyes, the better understanding they would get with their hearts.

"Make the heart of this people calloused; make their ears dull and close their eyes. Otherwise they might see with their eyes, hear with their ears, understand with their hearts, and turn and be healed."
Isaiah 6:10 (*Old Testament*)

How dangerously easy it is to neglect our hearts. We will become callous and we find no joy in living or serving. Life will seem hollow.

But, if our hearts are tender toward God, we can understand, and our gratefulness can flow through us to others.

Ironically, we can become so busy trying to do good that we lose our hearts for God (Matthew 13:15 *New Testament* "These people's hearts grow dull.").

So how is your heart?

# HYPOCRISY

What sin did Jesus condemn more than any other sin? Hypocrisy!

Religious hypocrisy is an unspiritual shame. Those who are trying to gain a reputation by playing the role of God lovers are unholy fakes who may fool people, but they cannot fool God. Be warned against the danger of "faking it."

I once saw a bumper sticker that read, "Jesus is coming – look busy." Although we may look busy, we cannot fool God about our faith, our character or our service.

Like the Pharisees whom Jesus denounced in

Matthew 23:13- 28 (*New Testament*), we may appear to be sincerely religious, but the Lord knows if our profession is merely a façade without saving trust or genuine devotion.

Are you a church-going hypocrite, depending on your own works to gain entrance into heaven? Or are you genuinely trusting in God's grace and relying on Christ?

You cannot fool God because He knows all and it is not enough to look busy. God sees and hears all our ways and he knows our hearts. We cannot hide or be camouflaged.

Be genuine before God, appealing to Him as David did in Psalm 51 (*Old Testament*):

"Create in me a pure heart, O God,
and renew a steadfast spirit within me.
Do not cast me from your presence
or take your Holy Spirit from me.
Restore to me the joy of your salvation
and grant me a willing spirit, to sustain me."

and "My sacrifice, O God, is a broken spirit;
a broken and contrite heart
you, God, will not despise."

# 11

# MEASURE YOURSELF

"Can you measure me today?"

Through their early years, my kids would call me to measure them to see how tall they were. Measurements are often indicators of growth, and it's always a good idea to measure spiritual growth.

Do you spend time reading God's Word and talking with him?

Do you look forward to fellowshipping with the Lord and His family, the church?

What fruit of the Spirit is apparent in my life? What isn't (yet)?

Do you talk about Jesus with people who don't

know him?

How are you using your spiritual gift(s)?

Do you have a generous and giving spirit?

How much better do you know God today than you did a year ago?

Your answers to these questions can be indicators of your own spiritual growth. A child seems to grow up all a sudden, but we know it's actually a slow, continual process. Measuring your growth isn't intended to focus on your shortcomings, but instead on your progress as your grow in your relationship with Jesus.

Just as Jesus grew in both wisdom and statue, as believers we are to continue to grow in both wisdom and statue. As believers we are to continue growing in the grace and knowledge of our Lord and Savior Jesus Christ (2 Peter 3:18 *New Testament*).

We are not to remain children, stunted in growth, but to grow up in all things into Him who is the head – Christ (Ephesians 4:14-15 *New Testament*).

May we heed Peter as he wrote: "Like newborn babies, crave pure spiritual milk, so that by it you may grow up in your salvation, now that you have tasted that the Lord is good." (1 Peter 2:2,3 *New Testament*)

Have you measured yourself lately?

# 12

# WEIGHED DOWN OR UP

If you get into a gas balloon basket, it has four sides. To get the balloon off the ground slowly, you release one sandbag at a time over the side, and the craft will start to ascend.

Apply this to your relationship with the Lord:

Once you become a Christian, understand that's when God begins to clean up your heart, so that you can get closer and closer to Him (Hebrews 12:1 and 1 John 2:15 *New Testament*).

Following the same spiritual principle, know that holding onto the world's ways (and the guilt of past sins) will weigh down your fellowship with the Lord.

In the Gospel of John (*New Testament*), Jesus taught that we cannot love the world and love God at the same time. How often we have proven from our own experience just how true that is.

Selfish attitudes, distracting sinful habits and worldly cares will keep us from getting off the ground spiritually. When we lay them aside with His help, we will experience uplifting joy and fellowship with the Father.

"Cast all your anxiety on him because he cares for you." (1 Peter 5:7 *New Testament*)

13

## WINNER

Everybody likes to be a winner. So when we read Romans 8:37 (*New Testament*),we learn that, as followers of Christ, we are more than conquerors. That is exciting. But what does that phrase really mean?

The apostle Paul began (in Romans 8 *New Testament*) by recounting God's grace in sending His son Jesus to die to pay the penalty for everyone's sins. He goes on to say that believers also have the help of the Holy Spirit to give them victory over the power of sin in daily life.

Some circumstances may make us feel alone and defeated, but in all situations he assures us that we are conquerors because nothing can separate us from the love of God which is in Christ Jesus our Lord.

You should think less of the power of things over you and more about what the power from having Christ in your life means for you.

# 14

# OVERCOMING RESISTANCE

If you've ever tried to water ski, you know how much the water resists you before you get up on the surface. The boats engine roars and your muscles strain to hang on while the water does everything it can to keep you down. But if you know how to take advantage of the boat's power, you will be lifted up and, within a few seconds, you are gliding over the surface of the same water that at first held you down.

Water skiing illustrates the experience as we go through the deep waters of trials. As believers, we must learn to take advantage of Jesus' power. At first, there is a great struggle and effort as we hang on with all our might, enduring momentary but no-less-challenging resistance to discover new levels of blessings and faith so we can overcome.

The resistance may seem almost unbearable, but, like the water that lifts us on skis, our difficulties can challenge us to depend on God's supernatural power.

The apostle Paul put it like this – "...we have this treasure in jars of clay to show that this all-surpassing power is from God and not from us." (2 Corinthians 4:7 *New Testament*).

Have we learned this amazing spiritual truth? Have you viewed the deep waters of trials as an opportunity to discover the supernatural power that can lift you up and then carry you over the waves of the same water that has successfully resisted you before?

If not, may you hold on and defy the resistance that has defeated you before only to discover a new spiritual victory and the hope He brings to your life.

# FOLLOW INSTRUCTIONS

After a woman sued a restaurant for being burned by coffee, companies started changing their menus and adding warning labels.

Look at these instructions on a frozen dinner: "Defrost before eating;" and, on an iron: "Caution, don't iron clothes on your body."

If some people need these obvious guidelines on household items, think about how much more we need God's direction.

In Proverb 6:27 (*Old Testament*), the inspired writer asks "Can a man scoop fire into his lap without his clothes being burned?

How often do we think we're the exception, only to get burned by life's "coffee?"

In Psalm 119:133-135 (*Old Testament*), we can read about the importance of God's "instruction manual:"

"Direct my footsteps according to your word;
let no sin rule over me.
Redeem me from human oppression,
that I may obey your precepts.
Make your face shine on your servant
and teach me your decrees."
and in 2 Timothy 3:16,17 (*New Testament*) Paul writes:

"All Scripture is God-breathed and is useful for teaching, rebuking, correcting and training in righteousness, so that the servant of God may be thoroughly equipped for every good work.

Ask God to teach you his direction. Read from and contemplate on the Bible often, and be wise enough to follow the instructions:

"Show me your ways, Lord, teach me your paths." (Psalm 25:4 *Old Testament*)

"I have considered my ways and have turned my steps to your statutes." (Psalm 119:59 *Old Testament*)

"For my thoughts are not your thoughts, neither

are your ways my ways," declares the Lord. Isaiah 55:8 (*Old Testament*)

"A person may think their own ways are right, but the Lord weighs the heart." (Proverb 21:2 *Old Testament*)

Ultimately, God wants us to believe Him and to believe on the Lord Jesus Christ. The result is our own salvation (Acts 16:31 *New Testament*).

He also wants us to be kind to one another, tenderhearted, forgiving one another, even as God in Christ forgave us (Ephesians 4:32 and Colossians 3:12-15 *New Testament*).

And He challenges us to go into our world and share the very good news of Jesus with every one (Mark 16:15 *New Testament*).

# 16

## DRINK

In 1989, a pastry shop in Maryland advertised this special offer – "Buy one of our coffee cups for $4.80 and fill up your cup for 25 cents each time you visit."

The owners never expected that 21 years later four longtime customers would still be getting their cup of coffee every day for 25 cents.

You won't find many deals like that anymore.

But Jesus offered something far more generous to a woman at a well. He said, "Whoever drinks of this well water will thirst again, but the water that I shall give will become in him a fountain of life." (John 4:13-14 *New Testament*).

The woman at the well was ready to listen. None of her many personal relationships had ever filled up her emptiness like what Jesus offered her – water that would refresh her parched life and give her something more, the promise of eternal life.

That same promise is ours as Jesus said, "I have come that they may have life and that they may have it more abundantly." (John 10:10 *New Testament*)

God's grace and love come from His bottomless reservoir – so drink from the water He offers and you will never thirst again.

# HONESTY IS THE BEST POLICY

A salesman walked into a fast food restaurant, ordered and paid for two dinners to go. When his number was called, he picked up the bag and left. When he arrived at home he discovered his order wasn't in the bag. Instead it contained the restaurant's money from that day's business.

He immediately returned with the bag just as the manager was reporting the loss to the police. This involved a large sum of money, but, even though he probably could have gotten away with keeping the money, this customer was honest – a rarity these days.

If we decide to follow Jesus, we must be honest in

all things, large as well as small.

"So in everything, do to others what you would have them do to you..." (Jesus in Matthew 7:12 *New Testament*)

We sometimes wonder why Christians aren't having a greater spiritual impact on our world. Could it be that many believers are cheating, lying, stealing or just hurting any and everybody they can out of selfishness, and then rationalizing their actions?

Too often, dishonesty is the order of the day, even for those professing to follow Jesus. No wonder those yet-to-believe aren't impressed. More important still; honesty is what God demands and expects of us.

The apostle Peter said that we are to have honorable conduct (1 Peter 2:12-15 *New Testament*). Then he wrote that by doing good, a believer may well put to silence the ignorance of foolish men. Honesty is not only the best policy. It is God's policy.

18

---

# WILLING TO CHANGE

A major league baseball pitcher was having trouble. He started the season with a terrible record. After mid-season, things began to get better. He won four games in a row and suddenly became nearly unhittable. When asked what was different, he replied, "mechanics."

In other words, he had discovered and corrected a bad habit in his pitching motion. After realizing his problem, he practiced diligently to correct it. The next time he pitched, his winning streak started.

Do you recall the last time you tried to change a bad habit? It wasn't easy because you were comfortable with the old way and the new seemed awkward.

That's why we often hesitate to make needed changes. For example, maybe you use words you shouldn't or you're critical of people, instead of helpful, even encouraging.

It takes awareness and a conscious decision on our part and God's help to change. The apostle Paul said we are to present ourselves as slaves of righteous for holiness (Romans 6:19 *New Testament*). That's not easy, but we must make the effort. Let me encourage you to be willing to change.

"Watch the way you talk. Let nothing foul or dirty come out of your mouth. Say only what helps, each word a gift. Don't grieve God. Don't break his heart. His Holy Spirit, moving and breathing in you, is the most intimate part of your life, making you fit for himself. Don't take such a gift for granted. Make a clean break with all cutting, backbiting, profane talk. Be gentle with one another, sensitive. Forgive one another as quickly and thoroughly as God in Christ forgave you." (Paul in Ephesians 4:29-32 *New Testament*)

# SOFT WORDS

In Proverbs 15:1 (*Old Testament*), Solomon tells us that a soft answer turns away wrath. While it's true that a humble response to wrath typically will cause another person's anger to subside, it is equally true that some people will never be pacified. One thing's for sure – a harsh word will stir up anger.

Choose your words carefully, and do all you can to control what you say, especially when you become upset. Often it is best to walk away from a stressful situation than contribute your upsets to the mix. But, too often pride and fear of being disrespected push us into conflicts we don't really want, and almost always regret later.

The Lord advises that we prepare our heart and attitude so we are prepared emotionally for encounters where someone will attempt to take advantage of our fears and insecurities.

We need to remember that we are his servants, with the purpose of loving (not necessarily liking) everyone, including those we know to be our enemies.

Letting an enemy lead any encounter allows them to win. Allowing Jesus to lead us guarantees we win, and most often by revealing the power of love and grace.

"You have heard that it was said, 'Eye for eye, and tooth for tooth.' But I tell you, do not resist an evil person. If anyone slaps you on the right cheek, turn to them the other cheek also. And if anyone wants to sue you and take your shirt, hand over your coat as well. If anyone forces you to go one mile, go with them two miles. Give to the one who asks you, and do not turn away from the one who wants to borrow from you." (Jesus in Matthew 5:38-42 *New Testament*)

# THE VALLEY OR THE TOP OF THE MOUNTAIN

The key to surviving in this constantly changing life is to expect the unexpected, to remain steadfast above all, and to remember daily that God is firmly in control, even when everything indicates otherwise.

We all know the feeling of being almost "there" only to have a sudden shift of circumstances that alters everything and we feel that life is out of control.

Just like trying to get to the top of that Big Mountain in front of you and you're at the bottom in the valley looking up.

In the valley, people can always count on bad things to happen, like mayhem, killings and rape.

Sometimes we start to climb that big mountain. We make it halfway up, lose our footing and slide right back down to where we started.

But if you keep your eyes and heart focused on the summit and start climbing whenever you lose some ground, eventually you will reach the top. The more you climb, the stronger your faith becomes. God blesses that.

"Without faith it is impossible to please God, because anyone who comes to Him must believe that He exists and that he rewards those who earnestly seek him." (Hebrews 11:6 *New Testament*)

Some of us never get out of the valley because they are so used to being around the negativity that lives there. Consider the fresh air of something higher and better. Start climbing.

# KING ARTHUR

Arthur, as a young King, nervously explained himself to his Queen. He recounted how he mysteriously pulled a sword out of a stone, entitling him to become king. Then he shared, "I never wanted to be a king and since I now am, I have been ill-at-ease wearing my crown, until my eyes beheld you. Then for the first time I suddenly felt I was King. I was glad to be King. Most of all I wanted to be the wisest, most heroic and most splendid King whoever sat on any throne."

His wife brought about a change in character and purpose. As we reflect on our beloved, the Lord Jesus, we experience a transformation.

Paul wrote, "We all, with unveiled face, beholding as in a mirror, the glory of the Lord, are being transformed into the same image from glory to glory by the Spirit of the Lord." (2 Corinthians 3:18 *New Testament*)

There is a mystery involving his life and our, his holiness and our former brokenness.

" I have been crucified with Christ and I no longer live, but Christ lives in me. The life I now live in the body, I live by faith in the Son of God, who loved me and gave himself for me." (Galatians 2:20 *New Testament*)

# 22

## LOSE OR GAIN

On my uncle's farm there were certain fields he sowed by hand. He would strap on a canvas contraption that looked somewhat like a kangaroo pouch, fill it with seeds and go out to sow. He would cast seeds everywhere.

When my uncle was sowing seeds in his field, it looked like he was throwing them away. They seemed to be lost but weren't really gone. In time, he would get get back a harvest far more than I ever anticipated.

When we give ourselves to Christ, it may seem to people as if we are throwing our lives away. But, he said that it is only as we lose our lives in him that we find true life (Matthew 10:39 *New Testament*).

Jesus taught us to measure our lives by loss rather than gains – by sacrifices rather than self-preservation, by time lavished upon others, and by love poured out rather than love poured into us.

It is a rule of life – God blesses those who give of their lives and resources (2 Corinthians 9:6 *New Testament*). Give away the truth you know and He'll give you more to give away. Give your time and you'll have more time to give, set no limit on your love and you'll have more love for others.

"The world of the generous gets larger and larger; the world of the stingy gets smaller and smaller." (Proverbs 11:24 *Old Testament*). It's one of the oldest paradoxes in the world but it's true.

# 23

# SILVANA – MY EVANGELIST

When my daughter Silvana was 7, she and I were talking in the front yard when two new neighbor kids stopped by. After I asked them their names, Silvana's first question to them was, "Do you love God?"

I just looked at her! Kathy, an 8 year old girl answered, "I don't know."

Silvana gave her a look of disapproval and concern. When 7 year old Samantha noticed Silvana wasn't happy with how her older sister had answered, she said, "Yes."

Silvana's witnessing strategy might not have been the most effective, but she did have an important question for the people she met (and I've heard her ask it of several others, as well).

Jesus was asked which was the first commandment of all (Mark 12:28-30 *New Testament*). He answered, "The Lord is one and you shall love the Lord God with all your heart and soul and all your mind and with all your strength." Jesus was referring to the pivotal times in the past when God had told the Israelites to place Him as the one and only God in their lives.

Loving God is to be our top priority. So, Silvana wants to know, "Do you love God?"

# 24

# THE COMEBACK

Who isn't inspired by one who makes a comeback after being down and apparently out of the race, the runner who stumbles and falls but then gradually moves up on the pack and into the lead?

The same kind of inspiration motivates Christians who draws courage from the example of our Lord and Savior.

No one was ever more humiliated than Jesus before he made his comeback. He was abandoned by his longtime friends and followers, insulted, mocked, falsely accused, spit on, whipped, stripped, beaten and nailed to a cross. While suffering and dying, a spear was thrust into his side. The executioners confirmed their success and declared Jesus dead. How can anyone be more down and out than that? Yet, that was not the end! Three days later, Jesus rose from the grave. He was the victor in his struggle over death, over sin and over hell.

Are you feeling out of the race today? Have you stumbled badly? Then look at Jesus' suffering and his resurrection. Just imagine what he has to offer you. No matter how far down you are now, the Lord is in your corner.

# DO YOU HEAR?

Do you have a child who seems to hear you only when they want something? Do they hear the first time you ask them to, please, bring something to you? Or do they seem to hear you only the second time when you put emotion into it? You may have to ask them even three times.

The apostle Peter was like that. Remember his after breakfast conversation with Jesus by the Sea of Galilee? As they talked, Jesus asked Peter three times if he loved him. Later, God repeated an important message to Peter three times (Acts 10:13-16 *New Testament*). From what we know Peter was a man who was hard to convince.

In my life I know I've been hardheaded and resistant to God's pleas to me. I finally figured I was simply wasting time getting into action, changing into a man who others could see was closely related to His son.

Are you similarly hard for God to convince of needed change?

# EQUIPMENT

In the church, there are spiritual leaders whose job is to equip us for ministry. In Paul's letter to the church in Ephesus, he wrote about equipping the people for service (Ephesians 4:11- 12 *New Testament*).

The Greek word used there for "equip" is the same one used to describe the disciples mending of their fish nets when Jesus called them into service (Mark 1:16-20 *New Testament*).

For three years Jesus mended holes in their ministry nets so they could be effective fishers of men.

If you don't know how to get started in finding and participating in a ministry, watch for people who can show you how it's done. Observe the way they learn and use the truths in the Bible, pray, and work with people, so the Lord can use you more effectively in the lives of others.

# MAKING A DIFFERENCE

Do you sometimes feel that your life isn't making any impact for God? The human race now numbers more than 10 billion people, the majority of whom don't know Jesus. This world's problems are overwhelming.

My praying, witnessing, and giving seems to be doing little to change our ungodly world. That's what I think, but that's not really the point. Our duty in life is to live each moment in fellowship with God. That means we don't let anything in our lives interrupt that fellowship. Our close relationship with God is at stake.

Are you facing a difficult, faith-stretching circumstance today? Your joyful obedience to God can be an encouraging example to others. You can become a follower of Jesus so that you are an example to all (1 Thessalonians 1:6-7 *New Testament*).

Also know that anything you do for Jesus makes a difference, whether you see it or not.

"Therefore, my dear brothers and sisters, stand firm. Let nothing move you. Always give yourselves fully to the work of the Lord, because you know that your labor in the Lord is not in vain." (1 Corinthians 15:58 *New Testament*)

# 28

# OVERFLOWING

When a cup is filled to overflowing, whatever spills over the edge is the same as what is being poured in.

But in our spiritual lives when this happens, there is a supernatural process occurring that is beyond our understanding.

If suffering is poured into a Christian, the Christian will overflow. But what spills over is different from what is poured in. Suffering goes in but comfort comes out. The Law of Flow and Overflow is spoken in 2 Corinthians 1:5 (*New Testament*). God will transform it by His supernatural grace and power. One translation reads, "Just as the suffering of Christ flowed over into our lives also through Christ, our comfort overflows."

When trouble flows in, look to God for His overflowing comfort.

# LIFE CHANGES

Our world is always in constant change. But God is not. Too often, the world seems to be trembling beneath our feet. God is the rock that can't and won't be shaken. In His Word He promises, "I am the Lord, I do not change." (Malachi 3:6 *Old Testament*)

On those occasions when we must endure life-changing personal losses that leave us breathless, there is a "place" we can turn to for comfort and assurance. We can turn to God. When we do, our living God stands ready to protect us, comfort us, guide us and, in time, to heal us.

Are you facing difficult circumstances or unwelcome changes? If so, please remember that God is much bigger than any problem you may face. Instead of fruitlessly worrying about life's challenges, put your faith in the Father and His son Jesus Christ.

"Therefore I tell you, do not worry about your life, what you will eat or drink; or about your body, what you will wear. Is not life more than food, and the body more than clothes? Look at the birds of the air; they do not sow or reap or store away in barns, and yet your heavenly Father feeds them. Are you not much more valuable than they? Can any one of you by worrying add a single hour to your life?" (Jesus in Matthew 6:25-27 *New Testament*)

Jesus Christ is the same yesterday, today, and forever (Hebrews 13:8 *New Testament*). Remember that fact. Life is always challenging, but, as Christians, we should not be afraid. God loves us and He will protect us in times of hardship. He will comfort us, He will guide our footsteps; when troubled or weak or sorrowful, God is always with us. We must build our lives on the rock that cannot be moved, we must trust in God always.

"Therefore everyone who hears these words of mine and puts them into practice is like a wise man who built his house on the rock. The rain came down, the streams rose, and the winds blew and beat against that house; yet it did not fall, because it had its foundation on the rock. But everyone who hears these words of mine and does not put them into practice is like a foolish man who built his house on sand. The rain came down, the streams rose, and the winds blew and beat against that house, and it fell with a great crash." (Jesus in Matthew 7:24-27 *New Testament*)

Take your troubles to Him. Seek protection from the one who can't be moved. God will protect you if you ask Him; so ask Him, and serve Him with willing hands and a trusting heart.

"Though an army besiege me,
my heart will not fear;
though war break out against me,
even then I will be confident...
For in the day of trouble
he will keep me safe in his dwelling;
he will hide me in the shelter of his sacred tent
and set me high upon a rock.
(Psalm 27:3, 5 *Old Testament*)

"The Lord is my rock,
my fortress and my deliverer;
my God is my rock, in whom I take refuge,
my shield and the horn of my salvation,
my stronghold."
(Psalm 18:2 *Old Testament*)

# ACCEPTING THE PAST

Some of life's greatest roadblocks are not the ones we see ahead but are instead the roadblocks that fill our rearview mirror.

We are imperfect people who lack perfect control over our thoughts. We allow ourselves to become stuck in the past. Even though we know better, we allow painful memories to fill our minds. We simply can't seem to let go of our past. Instead, we relive it again and again.

Thankfully God has other plans. In Philippians 3:13,14 (*New Testament*), Paul gives instruction to focus on the future, not the past. Yet for many of us, focusing on the future is difficult indeed, because we're fixated too intently on past failures and losses. Instead, we need to focus on more urgent matters, like accepting God's forgiveness, and being willing to forgive others today.

A crucial truth about forgiving is hiding in plain sight in what many know as "The Lord's Prayer" lifted up by Jesus in Matthew 5:12 (*New Testament*) – "and forgive us our sins, as we have forgiven those who sin against us."

Until we thoroughly and completely forgive those who have hurt us or until we completely forgive ourselves for our own mistakes and shortcomings, we will never be fully free from the past.

Once you have made peace with your past and those who have wronged you, you will be free to become fully engaged in the present. And when you become fully engaged in the present, you're then free to build a better future for yourself and those you love.

If you've endured a difficult past, "Learn from it – don't live in it." Instead, build your future on a firm foundation of faith, love and forgiveness, trusting in your Heavenly Father.

Give all your yesterdays to God. Your Creator

intends to use you in wonderful, unexpected ways, but only when/if you let and trust Him. But first God needs you to make peace with your past. And He wants you to do it now, not later.

In times of need, I often share Psalm 27 (*Old Testament*) to encourage people who are going through a difficult time.

Look more closely at the psalmist's hope. His expectation was not necessarily deliverance from bad circumstances, but instead the hope of seeing the goodness of the Lord. That's something we can see even in times of trouble.

31

---

# TRADE OFFS

Life is full of trade-offs. Today's poor choices are a down payment on tomorrow's problems. It's all part of living with the law of God that says, "We reap what we sow." (Galatians 6:7 *New Testament*).

A woman was drinking and driving which resulted in her being stopped, jailed, charged and convicted.

The judge sentenced her to 15 years and suspended all but one year. The judge gave her this choice – 15 years in prison or house arrest for one year. The trade of was simple. Stay home and out of trouble for one year instead of going to prison for 15 years.

She chose one year of house arrest.

Then the woman went fishing and was driving on a suspended license to get to the fishing hole. She got pulled over and was taken to jail. That one fishing trip cost her many years of freedom.

What bad trade offs do you make? Do you reject God's mercy so you can enjoy sin?

In the Bible we can see many examples of trade-offs. Moses traded the Promised Land for an outburst of anger (Numbers 20:7-13 *Old Testament*). David traded his reputation for a night of passion (2 Samuel 11 *Old Testament*). Ananias and Sapphira traded life for some extra money (Acts 5:1-11 *New Testament*).

Facing temptations today? Never exchange fellowship. Don't give in. While here and vulnerable to all human frailties, he faced every temptation that you've faced, and he chose to trust God each time.

Follow him.

# GENUINE BELIEVER OR
# JUST CHURCH GOING

Over the years, I've learned that there are 2 kinds of Christians. One is "church going people." These people show up on Sundays to be seen and/or pretend to others that they are spiritually-minded. But what do they do during the rest of the week, Monday through Saturday? You rarely see them during the week, because they don't want to be seen being their real selves – wolves in sheep's clothing.

The second one is Christians who are giving their time to help others. They are at church and Bible study, fellowshipping, for sure. They're always learning, studying, helping others and giving generously of their time.

A Christian resists gossiping or talking behind other's backs. The reason I'm saying these things is that I've seen firsthand from people who say they're people of God, but will stab you in the back, put you down and talk "bad" about you. They use you for what you can give them.

We must simply put this reality in God's hands because He knows best and He will take care of the problem His way. The thing is, if you put this in God's hands and not your own hands, God will handle their ignorance and sins in a much better way then you could, and of course, it would also be the right way.

Sometimes it doesn't feel right right away because God's timing is not the same as ours. Just trust Him, move on and focus on being of the latter group.

# 33

# GENERATIONS

Every generation becomes shaken up about its young people. But the problems are the same in every generation, they don't really change.

See if you can figure what generation this is.

"The youth are rebellious, pleasure seeking and irresponsible. They have no respect for their elders. They spend their days in idleness and their nights pursuing sensual lust. They have no respect for authority nor for the traditions of the past."

Who said it? Plato in ancient Greece. You might have thought that he was writing about this generation, wouldn't you? You were younger once. So don't be distracted by this ongoing truth: Youth can't "get" what they haven't learned yet. Let God help you be patient while they learn some missing "life lessons." And focus on applying the lessons you've already learned.

# 34

# CHARACTER

We are inclined to think that everything that happens is to be turned into useful teaching. In actual fact, it's turned into something even better than teaching, namely "Character."

The mountain top is not meant to teach us anything. Getting there is meant to make us something.

"...we also glory in our sufferings, because we know that suffering produces perseverance; perseverance, character..." (Romans 5:3-4a *New Testament*)

It's a wonderful thing to be on a mountain with God. But a person only gets there so that he may later go down into the valley below the mountain top to help show those in danger to aspire to greater things and turn from "valley living." (Mark 9:2, 14-18 *New Testament*).

May your "character" be a blessing to those who live in your valley.

# HUGS!

It's a wonder what a hug can do. A hug can cheer you when you're blue. A hug can say "I love you so," or "I hate to see you go." A hug is "Welcome back again!" And, "Great to see you!" or "Where have you been?" A hug can soothe the pain and bring a little rainbow after a burdensome rain.

The hug! There's just no doubt about it. We surely couldn't survive without it. A hug delights, warms, and charms. It must be why God gave us arms.

Hugs are great for fathers and mothers, sweet for sisters, swell for brothers, and a favorite grandmothers. A hug can break the language barrier and make the dullest day seem merrier.

How long has it been since you shared the international message of a hug?

# 36

## TIME

Time is the enemy of love; the thief that shortens all our golden hours.

I have never understood why lovers count their happiness in days and nights and years. Our love can only be measured in our joys and tears.

## 37

# BORN AGAIN DREAM

I had a dream about a convict – a crown of thorns was on his head. He came gliding down the highway, he looked up at me and said, "Hey, don't you know me? Don't you remember my name or my crime? I was busted and convicted, strung up in my prime, when I came to help everyone do their time."

I tried to be cool but I was shaking, I couldn't walk, I couldn't see. I said, "But I'm not one of the faithful. Lord, so why have you come to me?"

"I mean maybe I'm not doing great. But I figured at least I was doing fine! I'm not a free man, I'm a do-as-I-please man. So what's all this talk about my time?

"You can climb the highest mountain, swim the deepest sea, and roll around naked in money, but you'll never be free. So I've come to assist you, if you're willing to learn, on how to let your light shine. I've had dozens of faces and names, so don't get stuck in competitive games, you just have to love everybody all of the time."

I said, "Lord I'm the one in prison and you know my back hurts all the time. My father is heartbroken and my little sister can't stop worrying and crying. Politicians steal, cheat me, and look at what you're asking me to feel. I'm sorry, I respectfully decline!

Then without a word, He touched my heart, I felt something crack apart, like a door that hasn't been opened in quite some time. I saw the earth and everyone on it. I saw the light all over me. The good in everybody, I saw it the way that He must see. I felt His love for it all and how He sees every sparrow fall, and how sorrow always has its reason and rhyme. I let my hands fall to my side, and I cried and cried.

He said, "Now let's take it from the top about doing your time. If you don't have a cross it won't work! You have to seek if you want to find. I have a song I want to share it. I'll try to be simple and try to be kind. I won't get too carried away, by the things that pass every day. Try to keep peace in your heart and mind."

That's the entire Gospel at this time. Just love everybody all the time!

# VICTORY OVER ANGER & BITTERNESS

A self-centric life brings a lot of disappointment, and eventually a lot more anger and bitterness, because the world and people never delivers everything you want the way you want it.

To overcome any anger and bitterness you may have accumulated along the way, and defeat disappointment, you will need to take an alternate path instead of living for self. Along the way, you will need to:

1. Forgive others just as God forgives you (Psalm 103:12 *Old Testament* and Colossians 3:13 *New Testament*)

Choose to not dwell on the wrong done against

you and instead redirect your thinking so it is more Christ-like (Philippians 4:8 *New Testament*)

2.. Stop focusing on, gossiping about and "bad mouthing" people who have wronged you (Hebrews 10:17; Ephesians 4:29 *New Testament*)

Removing reminders of wrong done is one way to move on. (Jeremiah 4:1 *Old Testament*; I Thessalonians 5:22 *New Testament*). Seeking reconciliation with God and those who wronged you eliminates huge roadblocks. (I John 1:9; 2 Corinthians 2:7-11; Ephesians 4:26,27 *New Testament*)

3. Intentionally deal with each anger-provoking situation, taking into consideration the following:

• Identify the things that indicate you are getting angry, so you can be better prepared to manage your emotions;

• Immediately seek God's perspective (Genesis 50:20 *Old Testament*; Luke 23:34; Romans 12:1,2; Ephesians 4:30-32 *New Testament*)

• Realize that irritation is likely a signal that you need to change (2 Timothy 2:23-26 *New Testament*)

• Your heart is revealed by how you react (Deuteronomy 8:2 *Old Testament*; James 3:14-18

*New Testament*)

• Realize that you don't have to respond to every verbal attack. Silence is an option that may make you look smarter than you are (Proverb 17:28 *Old Testament*)

• Your peace and joy should be in the Lord and not dependent on other persons or circumstances in your life (John 14:1-3 *New Testament*)

• Confess all sinful thoughts. Pray and ask for God's help! (1 John 1:9 *New Testament*)

• Be quick to listen – ask questions, get the facts, make no presumptions or hasty decisions (Proverbs 18:13, 15 *Old Testament*; James 1:19a *New Testament*)

• Be slow to speak – seek God's solutions to any conflict or problem. Speak only edifying words to the other person – no more tearing down, and speak the truth with a gentle and quiet spirit (Proverb 15:1 *Old Testament*; Ephesians 4:15, 29; James 1:19b *New Testament*)

• Be slow to anger – attack the problem, not the person (Proverb 16:32 *Old Testament*; James 1:19c *New Testament*)

4. When dealing with someone else, focus on

their actions not their motive (Matthew 12:36-37 *New Testament*)

5. When dealing with yourself, focus on your heart, then change your actions (Matthew 12:34-37, 15:19; Hebrews 10:22 *New Testament*)

3. Actively put off your old self and put on a new self (Ephesians 4:22, 24 *New Testament*)

By being quick to listen, slow to speak and slow to anger, and in taking the alternate path, you are being renewed in the spirit of your mind (Ephesians 4:23 *New Testament*).

The difference will amaze you (and others who know the old you).

39

# WISDOM

It can't be found by seeking, but only seekers will find it. Wisdom cannot be communicated. The wisdom which a wise person tries to communicate usually sounds foolish. Knowledge can be communicated, but not wisdom. One can find it, live it, be fortified by it, do wonders through it but one can rarely communicate and teach wisdom.

Wisdom can't be put into words, it has to be experienced. That's the main difference between wisdom and knowledge.

Wisdom and joy come mostly from learning how to see a wider, much more wondrous world. And it's obvious most people aren't looking for wider, more wondrous view of things. Most people are narrowing their focus to what they want and how to get it.

The truth is revealed in the timeless Word of God.

"Blessed are those who find wisdom,

those who gain understanding,

for she is more profitable than silver

and yields better returns than gold.

She is more precious than rubies;

nothing you desire can compare with her.

Long life is in her right hand;

in her left hand are riches and honor.

Her ways are pleasant ways,

and all her paths are peace.

She is a tree of life to those who take hold of her;

those who hold her fast will be blessed."

(Proverb 3:13-18 *Old Testament*)

"For wisdom is more precious than rubies, and nothing you desire can compare with her." (Proverb 8:11 *Old Testament*)

"For since in the wisdom of God the world through its wisdom did not know him, God was pleased through the foolishness of what was preached to save those who believe." (1 Corinthians 1:21 *New Testament*)

"It is because of him that you are in Christ Jesus, who has become for us wisdom from God - that is, our righteousness, holiness and redemption." (1 Corinthians 1:30 *New Testament*)

And most amazingly, a New Testament writer reveals, "If any of you lacks wisdom, you should ask God, who gives generously to all without finding fault, and it will be given to you." (James 1:5)

ESCAPE FROM THE BAD LIFE

# 40

## ALTERNATIVES

In India, monkey hunters hollow out a hole in a coconut and put sweet candies inside. The hole is just big enough for the monkey to squeeze his empty hand into, but not big enough to get a fistful of candies out.

They stake the coconut into the ground. The monkeys find it and reach into it to get the candy, but then they're stuck. They have only two alternatives; hang onto the candy and be captured or let go and be free. Time and time again, even though they never get to eat it anyway, the monkey refuses to let go of their attachment to the candy.

The illusion of how good it would taste makes

them get caught and killed.

How many times, in our lives do we do the same thing? How many times a day?

Think (and let go).

# CIRCUMSTANCE

"I am not saying this because I am in need, for I have learned to be content in whatever the circumstance. I know what it is to be in a great need and I also know having plenty. I can do everything through Him who gives me strength." (Philippians 4:11-13 *New Testament*)

"But when He, the Spirit of Truth, comes He will guide you into all truth. He will not speak on His own, He will speak only what He hears and He will tell you what is yet to come. He will bring glory to you by taking from what is mine and making it known to you." (John 16:13, 14 *New Testament*)

"And we know that in all things God works for the good of those who love him, who have been called according to his purpose."

"What, then, shall we say in response to these things? If God is for us, who can be against us? He who did not spare his own Son, but gave him up for us all – how will he not also, along with him, graciously give us all things? Who will bring any charge against those whom God has chosen? It is God who justifies. Who then is the one who condemns? No one. Christ Jesus who died – more than that, who was raised to life – is at the right hand of God and is also interceding for us. Who shall separate us from the love of Christ? Shall trouble or hardship or persecution or famine or nakedness or danger or sword?

"No, in all these things we are more than conquerors through him who loved us. For I am convinced that neither death nor life, neither angels nor demons, neither the present nor the future, nor any powers, neither height nor depth, nor anything else in all creation, will be able to separate us from the love of God that is in Christ Jesus our Lord. (Romans 8:28, 31-35, 37-39 *New Testament*)

# 42

## AFTER A CRISIS

Perhaps you have picked up this book during a time of personal crises. If so, you have turned to the right place.

Each day offers the opportunity to learn from and praise our creator, God or to ignore or to rebel against Him. When you worship God with your prayers, words, thoughts and actions, you will be blessed by the personal relationship He wants to have with you.

Today and every day after it, there will be fresh opportunities for spiritual growth. If you choose, you can seize those by obeying God's Word, seeking His will, and walking with His son and our Savior, Jesus.

If you choose to begin your life "after crisis" in such a restoring, hopeful and empowering relationship, here are a few emphatic encouragements:

• Learn the lessons, and make the changes. God knows best. Accept that fact and His ways as fast as you can. Don't loiter. (Proverbs 3:5-8, 9:9 *Old Testament*).

• Remember that healing continues after the crisis has passed (Psalm 27:14 *Old Testament*).

• Get connected and get involved as soon and as much as possible. No back row sitting. (1 Thessalonians 5:11 *New Testament*).

• If a problem recurs, you'll now be better prepared when it does (Hebrews 12:1-3 and 11 *New Testament*).

• Share what you've learned (Titus 2:7; Philemon 6,7 *New Testament*).

• God has a plan and a path for you. Keep searching for that plan and keep following His path (Psalm 32:8 *Old Testament*).

At the end of the day, when no one else can comfort you, God can. God offers a peace unlike any other.

If you're like most of us, finding God's peace isn't

always easy, especially with a broken or hardened heart. But God has thousands of years practice healing and softening hearts far worse off than yours.

So, if you're struggling to find answers to life's toughest questions, don't give up.

Keep searching, starting with God's Word. There you'll discover strength and assurance that only God can provide, along with hope in abundance.

"To [those] who had believed him, Jesus said, 'If you hold to my teaching, you are really my disciples. Then you will know the truth, and the truth will set you free.'" (John 8:31, 32 *New Testament*)

"I have told you these things, so that in me you may have peace. In this world you will have trouble. But take heart! I have overcome the world." (John 16:33 *New Testament*)

# EPILOGUE

Your life may be rewarding, full of short-term treasures and pleasures. But one day (today?) you may just realize that it's headed somewhere you don't want to go, and you may become unfulfilled and restless.

In this book, I'm hoping to point you to the Map of Life that is God's Word – His way for His people to discover what He made them for, what He made you for – a path for a life that is alive with purpose.

But what do I know. I'm no longer a cool gangster. I'm just an ex-con with an escape story. What's next for you?

ESCAPE FROM THE BAD LIFE

www.ingramcontent.com/pod-product-compliance
Lightning Source LLC
LaVergne TN
LVHW091156080426
835509LV00006B/722